Grand Rive

6/12 10x L 3/11   08/17 13x L 4/16

Grand River

Jim Bedford and Tony Pagliei

Frank Amato

PORTLAND

River Journal

Volume 7, Number 2

Jim Bedford grew up in the Grand River Basin and has been fishing its waters for almost 50 years. He is an extremely avid river angler who especially loves to fish for steelhead, brown trout and smallmouth bass. Now retired from his day job as an environmental toxicologist he continues to teach angling classes at Lansing Community College. He has written for Outdoor Life, Field & Stream, Trout, Salmon Trout Steelheader, and numerous state and regional magazines. Jim has also written two other books, Steelhead Savvy and Flyfisher's Guide to Michigan.

Tony Pagliei was introduced to the sport of fly fishing and the art of fly tying along the shores of Lake Erie and Lake Ontario in Western New York over 25 years ago. Since his arrival to Michigan in 1992, he has spent thousands of hours fly fishing and guiding on the Grand River. Tony teaches fly tying and fly casting classes at the local fly shops and lectures at Michigan State University and Lansing Community College. He is a free-lance writer—with appearances in Fly Tyer, and Warmwater Flyfishing—and a video author as well, having written Tying Flies for Golden Bones. When the snow begins to pile up during the winter months, Tony commercially ties his warm water fly patterns for several fly shops and builds custom fly rods.

◆

Acknowledgments

Many thanks to Miles Chance who planted the seed for this book, Bob Brace and Jeff "Bear" Andrews for their fly contributions, and Kurt Hylek and Bob Bussinger for their angling and photo assistance. Thanks also to DNR fisheries biologist Jim Dexter and his staff who are always ready to answer questions about fishing the Grand River watershed.

◆

Series Editor: Frank Amato
Kim Koch

Photography: Jim Bedford and Tony Pagliei (unless otherwise noted)
Fly plates photographed by: Jim Schollmeyer
Design: Jerry Hutchinson

Softbound ISBN: 1-57188-277-4; Hardbound ISBN: 1-57188-278-2
(Hardbound edition limited to 350-500 copies)

Frank Amato Publications, Inc.
P.O. Box 82112, Portland, Oregon 97282
(503) 653-8108
Printed in Singapore
1 3 5 7 9 10 8 6 4 2

Grand River
Headwaters to Lansing

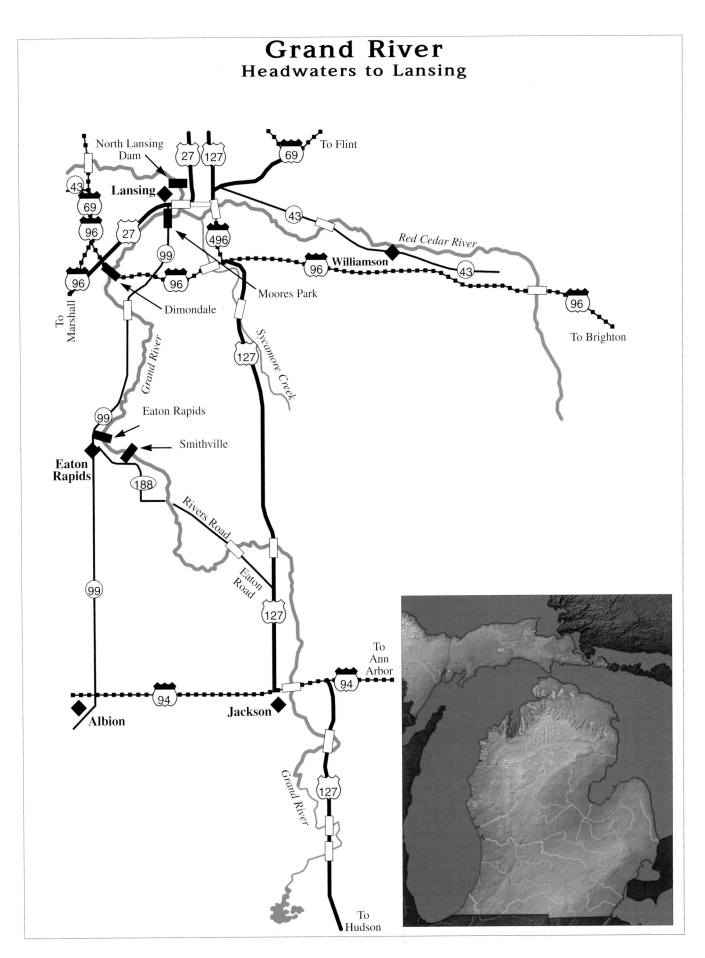

North Lansing Dam

27 127 69 To Flint

43

Lansing

69

96 27

99

To Marshall

96 96

Dimondale

Moores Park

496

96 Williamson Red Cedar River

43

43

96

To Brighton

Sycamore Creek

127

Grand River

99

Eaton Rapids

Smithville

Eaton Rapids

188

99

Rivers Road

Eaton Road

127

To Ann Arbor

94

94

Albion Jackson

127

Grand River

127

To Hudson

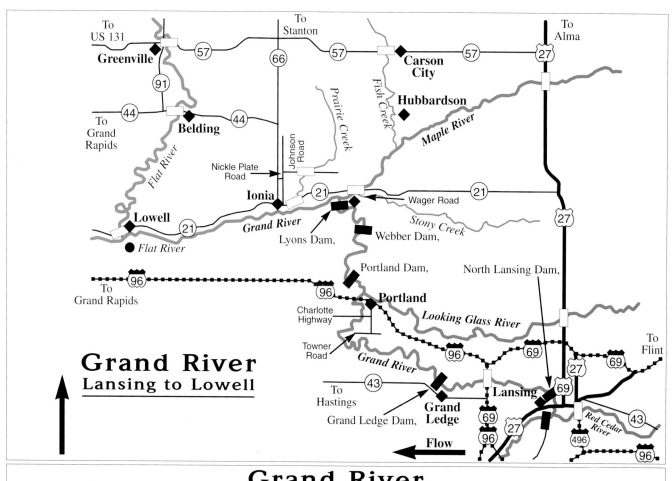

Grand River
Lansing to Lowell

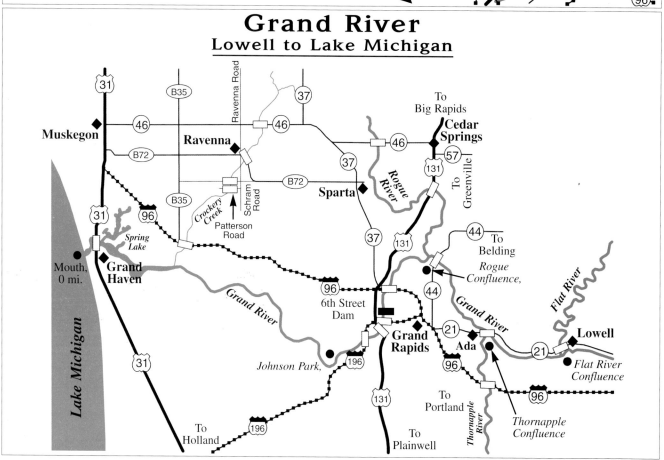

Grand River
Lowell to Lake Michigan

Grand River System

◆

The Grand River in southern Michigan has been my home river for more than 50 years. I still have vivid memories of pedaling my bicycle as a young boy to the Red Cedar River, a major tributary to the Grand that was less than a mile from my parent's house. When I was 11 a smallmouth bass of very large proportions for a river bass grabbed my night crawler rigged on a harness. After what seemed to be an eternity, I wrestled the bronze fish onto the bank. That smallmouth measured 20 and 1/2 inches and remains the largest smallmouth bass of my fishing life.

While the river was my childhood playground and a special place, all was not always well. I witnessed in agony several fish kills due to toxic discharges and dissolved oxygen depletions from rain following dry weather periods that washed waste with a very high oxygen demand from catch basins into the river. Toilet paper clinging to your line was a constant nuisance and in some years weed growth from the heavy nutrient load choked the river and made it virtually unfishable.

Fast forwarding to a few years ago finds me standing in the same reach of the Red Cedar in March battling my first steelhead on a fly. My fly fishing mentor and partner is Tony Pagliei and I had just watched a bright-colored male steelhead move out of the deep riffle and inhale his version of an albino egg-sucking leech. While I have dabbled with fly fishing in the past, most of my fishing has been with a spinning rod. Following retirement in 1998 from my day job as an environmental toxicologist I've been doing a lot more fishing with the fly rod and Tony has been very helpful when I have had questions or needed a special fly. He is a guide on the Grand River specializing in fly fishing for smallmouth bass, carp, steelhead and salmon. Tony is also a professional fly tier and an avid fly fisher. He will be contributing the fly, hatch, and tactics sections of this volume and his fly fishing expertise will be weaved in throughout.

A steelhead in the Red Cedar represents the fact that the good ole days of fishing in the Grand River watershed are occurring as you read this. Pollution control since the enactment of the Clean Water Act has greatly improved the water quality of the river and the fish have responded. The smallmouth bass is the primary resident game fish of the mainstream and many of the tributaries. Walleye, northern pike, channel and flathead catfish, and carp also provide great fly rod sport in the mainstream. These fish, along with brown and brook trout, are also found in the Grand's tributaries. When the water temperature of the Grand cools in the fall coho and chinook salmon, steelhead, lake and brown trout join the resident fish.

∾ The Mainstream ∾

All of Michigan's rivers drain into one of the Great Lakes. For that reason the majority of its rivers are rather short. The Grand River is Michigan's longest. It begins south of the city of Jackson and flows north and then west for about 250 miles to Lake Michigan. The river actually begins closer to Lake Erie but meanders to the west instead.

The Grand begins as a very slow-moving stream and continues this way for about 30 miles. The low gradient results in a soft bottom making the river difficult to wade. The river is floatable but the fishing is only fair with northern pike, walleye, and largemouth and smallmouth bass the principle game fish. As the Grand nears the small town of Eaton Rapids it begins changing to a classic smallmouth bass stream. It widens, the flow quickens, the bottom firms up, and boulders poke their round tops above the surface of the water. Eaton Rapids was named for the character of the river here and proclaims itself as the "only Eaton Rapids on Earth."

Except for where it is impounded, the Grand continues to alternate riffles with pools and contains boulder-strewn runs all

Tony battling a Red Cedar steelhead.

Tony Pagliei reaching for a smallmouth.

the way to the city of Grand Rapids. This is the prime fly fishing reach of the river. Most of the dams on the river are relatively low head, but three hydroelectric dams (Smithville, Moores Park, and Webber) do create substantial backwaters. The areas below each dam offer prime fly fishing opportunities. Access is good at each dam and there is usually a good concentration of fish below each barrier. The two main reasons for the increased numbers are the blockage of fish movement and the presence of disoriented or injured baitfish that have just passed over the dam or through its turbines. Of course anglers can also be concentrated at these locations and you may do better by trying stretches that receive less pressure.

Many road bridges provide additional access as do the developed public access sites with launch ramps which are shown on maps of the river. The Portland State Game Area, just upstream from the town of Portland, provides a number of additional access locations. Canoes and kickboats can be launched at many points where launch ramps are not present. You can exercise lots of smallmouth, with a few walleyes and channel catfish thrown into the mix. At normal summer flows you can also safely navigate the river in a float tube or a personal watercraft. If you like to cover lots of water, try launching at Charlotte Highway and then float through the entire state game area. The riverside park in Portland provides a good place to take out. Other prime floats in this section of the Grand include Fitzgerald Park in Grand Ledge to State Road or Jones Road to Turner Road.

Unless there is above normal rainfall, the Grand between Lansing and Portland remains quite clear in the summer. This really helps the fly angler, as you know the fish can see your offering. Smallmouth are the prime target in this reach but walleyes, channel catfish and rock bass are also present in good numbers. If you have not tangled with channel cats on a fly rod you are in for a very pleasant surprise. They will put just as deep a bend in your rod as smallmouth bass of equal size, and

Jim Bedford with a smallmouth from riffle.

they do not give up easily. Channels grow larger than smallmouth and often the chances are good that the huge smallmouth that broke your tippet was really a channel catfish. Smallies and rockies come to the surface for poppers as well as mayfly, damselfly and grasshopper patterns, but streamers imitating leeches, crayfish and minnows are best for big smallies, catfish and walleyes.

In the summer, the clear water of the upper Grand provides the opportunity for another special warm water fishery: sight fishing for common carp. These fish definitely use their eyes to feed and nymphs that imitate immature damselflies, mayflies, caddis flies and stoneflies, as well as crayfish patterns, will catch these large members of the minnow family. A stealthy approach and accurate casts are necessary for these surprisingly wary fish. Ten-pound fish can be expected and 20-plus-pound fish are possible. The common carp is known as the Golden Bonefish of the Grand, and with the vast population of these carp, finding them is not a problem on the Grand. Tony has been pioneering many new fly patterns and techniques over the past several years so hooking a carp on a fly is no longer a mystery.

I was fishing with Tony when I hooked a good-sized carp at the top of a run. Almost immediately the broad-backed fish managed to run my line around a stick that poked above the surface. I slacked off on the carp and started to wade over to free my line as I had done so many other times with various species of large fish. Within a few steps Tony literally shouted at me to break off the fish so that we wouldn't "spook the pool." Well, I think that was the first time ever that I didn't do everything I could to try to land a big fish. It was painful to point my rod at the snag and break the tippet but Tony knew best. We hooked another half dozen feisty carp in that pool before they quit hitting.

Duh...Dam Warning! Moore's Park, Lansing.

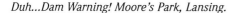

Plankton blooms and other biological activity in the impoundment behind Webber Dam and the turbid flow of the Maple River combine to decrease the clarity of the Grand's middle and lower reaches. This, along with generally deeper water, lowers but does not eliminate the dry fly opportunities and there is still great sport to be found below the surface. While smallmouth bass continue to reign, walleyes and channel catfish become more numerous as we move downstream. Flathead catfish become a real possibility as well. The areas below Webber and Lyons dams are very easy to wade during normal summer flows, but once the Maple River joins the Grand, floating becomes a better way to negotiate the river. Some of the Grand's most productive water can be fished by wading between the mouth of the Maple and Lyons Dam.

There are still many areas that can be waded to some extent downstream from the Maple but the river is often not crossable and wading from one access point in the river to another is difficult. One lower stretch of water that is very wadeable in the summer is the rapids for which the city of Grand Rapids is named. Downstream from the Sixth Street Dam, the 400-foot-wide river essentially becomes a giant riffle for more than a mile. There are some holes, such as the Quarry Hole where bedrock was blasted for construction material, but during usual summer flow rates the river is easily negotiated on foot. The bottom is uneven and the current can be strong so a wading staff is highly recommended. The water is fairly turbid in the summer and often you cannot see submerged rocks that are waiting to trip you up. Wading slowly while probing with your staff will keep you from taking a spill. Once the water clears in the fall the rocks becomes slippery with algal growth due to the better light penetration and felt or studded soles are a real good idea.

A number of city street bridges, along with their abutments, add structure and cover. In addition, there are four coffer dams ranging from one to three feet in height that provide

Releasing a golden bonefish on the Grand.

Snapping turtle near shore.

resting and feeding locations for fish. Smallmouth are still the dominant species but catfish and walleye are very numerous. This is probably one of the best places in the river for a fly angler to tangle with a large flathead that can weigh 30 pounds or more. There are public access sites on both sides of the river at the dam. River walks extend on each bank throughout most of the rapids. The only negative aspect to fishing these rapids is that instead of tree-lined shores you will be looking at a lot of bricks and concrete.

As the Grand gets closer to Lake Michigan it slows and deepens which changes the species mix a bit. Largemouth bass and northern pike become more numerous. There are bayous and side channels that are more like lakes than a river, and their inhabitants are the usual largemouth bass, pike, catfish, carp and a panfish mix you would expect to find in a warm water lake.

Prime months for the Grand River's resident fish are May through September although most species remain active into October until the water temperature falls below 50 degrees. Walleyes can be caught throughout the year but they will hit better when the water is above 45 degrees. The Grand's second season—the first in the minds of many anglers—begins as soon as the river water temperature cools into the 60s in late August or September.

There are five species of anadromous salmon and trout that run the Grand River System each year and we will discuss those fisheries after we describe the dam areas in greater detail and the Grand's major tributaries.

∽ Sixth Street Dam ∽

Before we describe the rapids below Sixth Street Dam in detail it is important to talk about water levels. During low flows all of the rapids are accessible to wading anglers but as the river rises, one must limit his or her wading to certain locations. There is a staff gauge on the ladder structure above the ladder

Steelheading below 6th Street Dam.

and there is a United States Geological Survey gauge in the lower rapids. It is important not to confuse the gauge above the ladder with the one in it. We will refer to the gauge readings above the ladder as we describe fishing in the rapids. When the river is very low, at about its base flow, the ladder gauge will read about 5.0 and the USGS gauge will be 3.0 feet. An even two-foot difference will be maintained up to 5.5 and 3.5 but then the depth starts to increase faster on the USGS gauge. (For example 3.7 equals 5.6, 3.9 equals 5.7, and 5.2 equals 6.0.) Once we get above 6.0 on the ladder gauge, the wading gets tougher as does the fly fishing. The USGS reading is available on the Internet (**http://wwwdmilns.er.usgs.gov**) but you must read the staff gauge at the ladder.

The prime fly fishing areas near the dam are Center Run and the Flats. The Flats are found on the eastern side of the river and are a shallow, fast sweep of water over bedrock just below the dam. The remnants of icebreakers on the dam delineate the center of the river. On the western side, the water is much deeper and the area near the dam is called the boils. You can fish the tail out of these boils if you can find space to fish. The Center Run is named for its location and it is where the main flow of the river occurs. There are three

slightly deeper areas or dips in the Center Run where the fish tend to lie and you will learn their locations as you fish it. The Center Run fishes best when the river level is between 5.4 and 5.7 but you can get out to it when the level is up to 6.0. It is usually fished from the western side but you can cross at the bottom end of the Center Run and wade up the middle of the river. The limit for doing this is about 5.8 for most anglers. This allows you to cover the Center Run in a different way and usually with less competition. From the middle of the river you can also fish a secondary run to the east that flows into the Quarry Hole. The Quarry Hole is too deep to effectively fly fish but you can find fish at times where it tails out near the I-196 Expressway crossing.

Just above the x-way there is a transverse trough that extends almost the whole width of the river. You can't wade through it but you can fish above and below it. After having shallowed up for awhile the Center Run deepens again as it joins the trough. It stays deep and fast as it flows along the western side of the second set of pillars from the eastern side of the river. There is also a transverse trough below the x-way that deserves your attention, especially in the center of the river. The first cofferdam influences the water below this trough, and while this area holds fish, it is often a bit difficult to find them in this non-descript water.

There is a large bridge (Bridge Street) between the first and second coffers and its abutments provide cover for both resident and anadromous fish. Wading can be tough here because of strong currents and an uneven bottom. Use your wading staff but don't try it if the water level is at 5.7 or above. There is also good holding water just above the second coffer. The area between the second and third coffers is relatively shallow with lots of food producing gravel. Fishing just below the second coffer and just above the third will be the most productive. You can easily wade back and forth across the river here when the water level is less than 5.5. The area just above the third

Fishing below 2nd Coffer Dam.

Author, Tony Pagliei, with a Grand River steelhead.

Bob Bishop with 10-pound laker.

Run. This run extends all the way down to an old railroad bridge (now a pedestrian bridge) and you can fish it from the center of the river, if the water level is less than 5.6, or roll cast from shore. The current is very strong here but fish hold well behind the submerged rocks that pepper this stretch of river. The good news for fly anglers is that the water runs only three to five feet in depth and fish have to make quick decisions as your nymph, egg fly, or streamer passes by them. Below this run there is some pocket water and a little bit of white water. As we reach Fulton Street there is good holding water along the abutments and under the bridge. The bedrock ends here and below the bridge the water deepens and soon becomes difficult to wade.

～ Lyons Dam ～

Access is available on each side of the river below the Lyons Dam. (Fish hold and feed near the dam and below the apron.) To fish the apron area below the dam it is best to enter the river from the eastern or ladder side. The bridge just below the dam also deserves lots of attention, especially the first two areas between pillars on the western side. Below the bridge, the main flow and deeper water is on the western side of the river. You can roll cast from shore, or wade out from the eastern side, when the water is not too high. This run angles to the center of the river and tails out below the power lines. Swinging streamers in the tail out is a good plan for both resident and anadromous fish.

Moderate depths, with lots of boulders, continue downstream for a few hundred yards. Then the river shallows into a long riffle. There is a lot of cover associated with this deep riffle and this stretch of gravel deserves to be looked over. Wadeable water continues below the riffle and spending time just below that point can be very productive. At low to moderate flows the Grand remains wadeable all the way downstream to the mouth of the Maple River, giving you another mile of good fishing water.

coffer fishes best when the water level is between 5.5 and 5.7 and fish seem to hold best above this coffer in the center of the river.

Another bridge is found between the third and forth cofferdams but its abutments don't attract fish as well as those of Bridge Street. There is a deep run along the walkway on the eastern side of the river that holds fish well but it will be a challenge to get your fly down to the fish. A much better run for fly fishing is found on the western side of the river between the bridge and the fourth coffer. The western half of the coffer dam is also an area to concentrate your efforts. The area above the coffer fishes really well at water levels between 5.3 and 5.6, but it quickly becomes tough to wade at higher levels. You can wade out and fish the run along the western shore at higher levels because there is little current for the first 30 feet out from the bank. Another bridge is found just below the fourth coffer and the best fishing is found just below the coffer and at the head of the abutments.

Downstream there is a large rock or concrete cluster in the center of the river that is painted with a fading blue paint (the blue rock) and a building that houses a carousel that extends out over the river on the western bank. In-between lies the Carousel

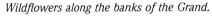

Wildflowers along the banks of the Grand.

Miles Chance enjoying solitude on the Grand

⌇ Webber Dam ⌇

There is a public access site on the eastern side of the river that can be reached from Maple Road and then Park Boulevard. A prime area to fish is below the cofferdam. When the water is relatively low, with only one turbine running on the dam, you can wade all the way across the river here and swing streamers or drift nymphs downstream, but you will need to return to shore to wade further downstream. An excellent run is found between the end of the wall that separates the turbines from the overflow gates down to a large island. Fish continue to hold all along both sides of the island as well.

Downstream from the island, when the two channels come back together, there is a prime gravel-bottomed run that extends for a considerable distance. Below this run it is best to be on the western side of the river. At low water you can cross just below the island before the two channels have completely combined. If it is too deep you can retreat to shore and walk further downstream. A prime spawning riffle is located a few hundred yards downstream at the mouth of Goose Creek. Fishing the runs above and below this spawning riffle will produce salmon in the fall, steelhead in the spring and walleyes, channels catfish and smallmouth bass in the summer.

⌇ Portland Dam ⌇

The ladder at the Portland Dam is on the south side of the river and there is a public access site there. The power channel can hold fish but the better fly fishing is found in the main river. At modest water levels you can walk downstream to where the channel tails out and cross it to the rocky main flow. From here, you can wade almost up to the dam. With a wading staff and great care you can cover most of the water below the dam.

Downstream the water is relatively shallow with lots of big rocks for a relatively short distance. Then the river starts to be influenced by the backwater of the Webber Power Dam. Fishing the transition from fast to deep water is a good plan, especially when you don't find fish in the shallow, faster stretches.

⌇ Fitzgerald Dam ⌇

Located inside of Fitzgerald Park in Grand Ledge, this dam is the most ideal site for the fly fisher. Under normal flows, water depths range from two to five feet. The deeper slots are located along the apron of the spillway. They vary from four to ten feet in depth and at times hold numerous smallmouth bass, walleye and catfish. On the western side of the dam is the Ole Dam Hole. This is a section of the original dam which is still in place. The new foundation was added with the addition of a fish ladder on the opposite side. This is the deepest pool below the entire dam and depending on the time of the year can hold several game fish species at a time. I have witnessed many fly anglers taking steelhead and salmon from this section as well. On the fish ladder side of the dam there is also a good-size pool

Tony Pagliei with a walleye at Fitzgerald Dam.

but it is located downstream about 50 feet from the ladder. Below this pool is a major run that is 50-yards long which sweeps along the park's edge. Migratory resident and non-resident fish stage and feed in this area prior to upstream movement. The entire layout of this dam site looks intimidating, but with the assistance of a wading staff, felt bottom waders and polarized glasses, the area below Fitzgerald Dam is excellent fly water.

⌇ Red Cedar River ⌇

The Red Cedar River joins the Grand in the city of Lansing and is the first major tributary to add its flow to the mainstream. The prime water for both resident and anadromous fish is between the town of Williamston and the river's mouth. A dam in Williamston has been modified to provide a short run of white water rapids for paddle sport enthusiasts and the entire stretch of the river is floatable by canoe or small boat. The Red Cedar can be easily waded at normal levels, except for a mile or two above a low head dam on the Michigan State University campus, and the last three miles above the confluence with the Grand, where the North Lansing Dam impounds the tributary. When floating in low water, you will have to walk your craft over the small dam on campus. It is also important to note that MSU has a local ordinance prohibiting fishing from the bank but this should not affect your fishing since wading or floating provides better casting room. This ordinance was also on the books when I was a youngster and yet I regularly fished from the bank. My childhood mentor, and frequent fishing partner, was a campus police officer so obviously the ordinance wasn't enforced then. The recent enforcement of the no fishing law seemed to coincide, though, with the arrival of salmon and steelhead on campus.

The principal resident game fish in the Red Cedar are smallies, rock bass and northern pike. All three species are found throughout the river with pike being more dominant in the slow, deep water and the bass preferring the rocks, stumps, and logs in more moderate currents. You may encounter walleye and channel catfish in the lower river that have moved up from the Grand. The insect species present are similar to the mainstream except for higher numbers of the Hexagenia mayfly. We haven't fished this hatch at night for smallmouth but these fish eagerly come to the surface for poppers and dry flies during the day. Streamers that imitate common shiners and creek chubs are very effective for pike when stripped in past weed edges and logs. Road bridges provide access and there is a county park where Grand River Avenue crosses the river and city parks in Okemos and Williamston. River walks in Lansing and East Lansing provide access to the lower river as well as the Grand.

Sycamore Creek joins the Red Cedar in Lansing and has a good population of northern pike with some smallmouth. This stream clears faster than the Red Cedar or the Grand following a rain shower so it can be a good backup to the larger rivers. Most of the lower third of the creek flows through mature woods so there is enough room for fly casting. Scott Woods and Biggie Munn parks in Lansing provide access in addition to the road crossings.

～ Looking Glass River ～

The Looking Glass River mirrors the Grand in that it begins as a sluggish, meandering, mucky-bottomed stream and then gradually the current begins to quicken and the stream widens as it proceeds downstream. Like the Red Cedar, the Looking Glass gathers its water from the east and north of the Grand River. Once the Looking Glass passes under U.S. 27 it has a firm gravel and cobble bottom with numerous large boulders. This is classic smallmouth water and the river maintains this

Late-winter snow and fresh steelhead on the Red Cedar River.

Looking-glass northern pike.

character all the way to its confluence with the mainstream in Portland. Rock bass and northern pike join the smallies in this reach and there are ample opportunities to fish for carp as well. While there are plenty of pike present in the large holes in the lower river they are more common upstream. Even though the upper river is quite deep and narrow, there is room to cast in the five miles or so of river above U.S. 27.

Relatively speaking, holes with adequate cover and depth for large fish are quite scarce in the lower Looking Glass. This is not necessarily bad news, because when you do find a good hole, it will be loaded with fish. The key is to cover a considerable distance of the river in order to fish a number of prime holding areas. County road bridges are conveniently located every mile or two, and fishing from bridge to bridge, whether wading or floating, is a good tactic. Many years ago several friends and I managed to fish all the lower sections of the Looking Glass and rated each bridge-to-bridge stretch relative to their holes and cover. This helped us focus on better water during subsequent trips. I would like to share the rating system with you now except, as we all know, rivers change and it might be very misleading.

You can expect multiple hook-ups in the good holes in the Looking Glass and fishing them in an upstream direction will increase your action. Try to steer your hooked smallies and pike downstream and out of the pool, if possible, so as to not spook the other fish. Sight fishing for carp is also more successful in an upstream direction as these fish are very wary.

～ Maple River ～

The Maple River is the next major tributary to the Grand, and again, it too joins the mainstream from the north. Even during dry weather, the Maple suffers from high turbidity due to the soil types in it drainage basin. This is really unfortunate for the fly angler because there is a good population of channel catfish along with some flatheads and walleyes. Pike and smallmouth

⌒ Terri Bedford with Coldwater Creek brown. ⌒

bass are also present. Despite the low visibility you can still have some success by slowly swinging and stripping oversized marabou streamers in the reach between Maple Rapids and the Grand. Make short casts, quartering downstream, and pulse the streamers almost in place with little forward progress.

If you have a difficult time enticing a strike in the muddy Maple you can try its two largest tributaries. Fish Creek and Stony Creek join the Maple just a short distance up from where the Maple enters the Grand River. Fishing the Maple at the mouths of these two large creeks can be productive.

Stony Creek is a very good smallmouth bass stream producing fish of remarkable size. The character of this small stream makes it relatively easy to fish with a fly rod. The rock-strewn pools are large and most of the creek flows through open farmland or mature wood lots. The first few miles above the Maple are best and you can access the creek at the M-21 and Wagar Road crossings.

Fish Creek is a bit larger and offers even more fly angling opportunities. The lower creek, between Carson City and the mouth, has a good population of smallmouth bass with an occasional northern pike or walleye present to grab your fly. Upstream from Carson City, the creek is regularly stocked with

yearling brown trout. These fish grow rapidly in this food-rich farmland stream. While overhanging vegetation can limit casting in some areas, most of the creek between Vickeryville Road and Carson City is fly-fishable.

This part of Fish Creek is now open all year for fishing but browns and brookies must be released outside of the regular trout season. I add brookies because there are wild brook trout in the headwaters of Fish Creek and some do drift down into the lower creek and are a very pleasant surprise when encountered. When I've caught a brookie in this water it is usually a good one. There is some natural reproduction of brown trout in the lower sections and good numbers of wild browns are present with the brookies upstream. The Holland Lake, Crystal, Sloan, and Senator Road crossings provide access to some of the better trout water.

A very prolific brown drake hatch occurs on Fish Creek, usually in late May. Brown trout feed heavily during this hatch. I've witnessed fish up to 26 inches in this stream and this hatch gives you a fine chance to hook a 20-inch brown on the surface while it is still light out. Crayfish are also very abundant in this stream and are an important food item for large browns. At times, as you are wading, the bottom almost moves with crayfish. But as you near a good hole they often disappear. The reason is lurking in the depths and the lack of crayfish a signal for you to fish the spot well.

Prairie Creek is neither a tributary of the Maple, nor is it a major tributary of the Grand, but it joins the mainstream just downstream from the Maple and deserves strong mention here. It is about the same size as Fish Creek and has a resident brown trout population that is supplemented with an annual stocking. Additional similarities include a good brown drake hatch and a healthy crayfish population.

Stream-resident brown on albino egg-sucking leech.

Steelhead successfully reproduce in Prairie Creek, and small rainbows will keep you busy when the browns are not taking. In addition, small percentages of steelhead parr do not smolt and become resident rainbows. I've caught several that measured up to 17 inches and they definitely spiced up the summer action. The brown trout grow at a good rate in Prairie Creek, and topping the magic 20-inch mark with a well-presented fly is always a possibility.

A couple of years ago I traveled to southwestern Montana and enjoyed some of the outstanding trout fishing for which that the area is famous. In a week, I landed several hundred browns and rainbows in the 12- to 19-inch range. My first outing when I returned home was to Prairie Creek. After a couple of hours, my only encounters were with creek chubs and small rainbows. Definitely back to Earth compared to the Montana trout heaven I had just experienced. But, then a big dark shadow glided out from an overhanging bush and I was in business. The brown measured 20 and 1/2 inches and weighed a full four pounds. As it swam from my hands, back to its dark lair, I thought that living in the Grand River watershed was still a pretty good deal. Despite prime trouting in Montana no 20 inchers were encountered. And in addition, in only a few

months, I would be duking it out with 30-inch rainbows, a.k.a. steelhead, in Prairie Creek. (More on the steelhead run later.)

⮜ Flat River ⮞

The Flat River joins the Grand in the town of Lowell and is a fine smallmouth bass stream. A special attribute of the Flat is that it is the slowest to muddy, and the quickest to clear, after a heavy rain on any of the Grand River tributaries. In addition, moderate rains don't seem to affect its fishability. This makes the Flat River your insurance policy when it rains hard and the other rivers are too muddy.

Even though the Flat is basically a warm water river, there is a chance to catch brook trout in it during the springtime. There are several small brook trout creeks north of Greenville that feed the Flat, and brookies up to 16 inches move down into the main river to feed. Usually the water temperature stays cool enough for them until late May. While traditional brook trout patterns catch these fish, remember that they have moved down to take advantage of abundant larger food items like minnows and crayfish in the Flat. So take advantage of this and use streamers that imitate prey items. Upstream from Langston, the bridges at M-⁁1,

Dennis Dann with a large, river smallmouth bass taken on a San Antonio Worm.

Lake Road, and Briggs Road provide access to the best water for these seasonal brookies.

The prime smallmouth water is between Greenville and the confluence with the Grand. The boulder-laden river offers perfect habitat for the bronzebacks except for where the Flat is impounded. The usual streamer patterns work well here and in the clear water the bass are frequently surface oriented so get out your poppers and buggy dries.

A number of years ago the Department of Natural Resources experimented with planting brown trout near the small town of Smyrna, south of Belding. Being the trout nut that I am, I fished this area hard during the year following the stocking. While I did catch a few carry over browns, it was the smallmouth fishing that was most impressive. The DNR soon discontinued the brown trout stocking, but the Flat above and below Smyrna continues to offer prime smallmouth fishing.

The Grand, at the mouth of the Flat, is wadeable when the water is low and is a prime smallmouth spot. You can also expect to catch some walleyes and channel cats here as well. The Flat near the confluence also offers good fishing.

～ Thornapple River ～

This tributary to the Grand is nationally known as a fine smallmouth bass stream. It is the only larger feeder stream that joins the Grand from the south. The Thornapple River suffers from too many dams especially in its lowers reaches. However, in the free-flowing sections between Nashville and the junction with Coldwater Creek you will find outstanding numbers of smallmouth bass. Your chances for larger than average size bass are also good here. Northern pike and rock bass, along with the occasional walleye, will add variety to your catch. Muskellunge

Large resident brown from tributary.

and largemouth bass inhabit Thornapple Lake, a natural widening of the river, and sometimes move up and down into the river. There are a number of small trout streams that add their flow to the Thornapple and during the spring and fall you may be surprised by a brown trout in the main river near their mouths.

Most of the free-flowing Thornapple can be waded or floated during normal summer flows, and there is good access at numerous county road crossings. A couple of good floats are from the Middleville Dam to Parmalee Road and from Parmalee Road to 100th Street. Streamers that imitate crayfish and creek chubs are again prime offerings for large smallmouth.

The largest tributary to the Thornapple, and the only trout stream in the drainage that is large enough to comfortably cast a fly in, is Coldwater Creek. Much of this stream has been dredged and straightened but it still offers good fishing for browns and an occasional rainbow. A number of Half Logs have been placed in the creek near Freeport and plans are in the works to add more stream-improvement structures to augment its relatively sparse cover. The go-ahead on this work took some doing by the DNR and Trout Unlimited because the stream is classified as a county drain. Usually the drain commissioner's goal is to keep the drain clean rather than allowing angler groups to add logs and other impediments to the flow.

Starting as a lake outlet and a warm water stream, Coldwater Creek cools off enough for trout about four-miles upstream from the town of Freeport and continues to hold trout almost to its confluence with the Thornapple. Downstream from Freeport the creek is open for fishing all year, but the browns must be released outside of the regular trout season from the last Saturday in April until the end of September. Growth rates are good in the creek, so the size limit has been raised to 12 inches in the upper creek. There is some natural reproduction but the wild fish are augmented with annual stockings of brown trout and, on occasion, rainbows.

There are many county road bridges for access to the Coldwater, as well as a county park at Morse Lake Avenue, and the Trout Unlimited property above Baker Avenue which is open to the public. Riffle loving insects predominate in this stream, with good hatches of caddisflies and blue-winged olive and Baetis mayflies. Crayfish and creek chubs are also abundant. Highbank, Cedar, and Glass creeks are smaller trout streams that join the Thornapple in Barry County near Hastings. They all can be plied with a fly rod to some degree but you will be mostly roll casting and some time will be spent with your fly in the hook keeper as you bust brush to make it to the next open area.

～ Rogue River ～

The Rogue River is the Grand's only large cold water tributary. Even though it is relatively marginal for trout, both browns and rainbows survive year-round in the lower river. Like Coldwater

Tributary brown on Woolly Bugger.

Creek, the Rogue begins as a warm water stream draining muck farms and gathering the outlets of small lakes. There are limited opportunities to fish for northern pike and an occasional brown trout in the section between M-46 and Pine Tree Avenue. The stream's real draw for fly anglers is the trout fishing from Algoma Avenue down to the confluence with the Grand. In this reach the river rapidly changes from a relatively narrow soft-bottomed stream to one that is broad with a firm gravel and sand substrate.

Prime trout water is found between the two Twelve Mile Road bridges. Here the river is easy to wade and offers the fly angler a fine chance to fool some sizable browns and rainbows. The nutrient rich Rogue has a large population of mayflies, with an especially prolific brown drake hatch usually occurring in late May. Other hatches include Hendrickson, blue-winged olives, white mayflies, sulphurs, and a modest Hexagenia emergence in June.

There is a small impoundment formed by a low head dam in Rockford. Trout seem to move back and forth between the impoundment and the shallow riffles above it. Even though the impoundment has a slight warming effect, trout survive the summer below the dam. Part of the reason for this is that additional springwater and small cold creeks add their water to the lower Rogue on its journey to the Grand. Smallmouth bass mix with the trout as we near the confluence and there is good walleye and smallmouth fishing off of the mouth of the Rogue. The wading is tough here but you can launch a boat just upstream from the Rogue mouth. Steelhead are a big deal in the Rogue and we will return to themwhen we describe the Grand's anadromous fisheries.

∽ Crockery Creek ∽

The first sizable tributary to enter the Grand upstream from Lake Michigan is Crockery Creek. It becomes fly fishable after its two branches join in Ravenna. Brown trout, along with some small rainbows that are destined to become steelhead, are present for the first few miles below Ravenna. The stream gradually warms and soon the trout give way to a modest population of smallmouth bass and pike. For those who like to test their skills, and don't mind some brush, the North Branch can still be fished upstream past the forks. Roll casting will be necessary most of the time but there is a large pastured area between Laketon Road and the forks that has more casting room. Again, like the Rogue, steelhead are a big draw in this stream and we will describe that fishery later.

∽ Hatches And Non-Hatches ∽

A very diverse aquatic insect community has developed in the Grand River system over the past several decades due to the nature of the watershed and its improving water quality. Even though the Grand is considered a warm water stream, many of the major aquatic insect hatches usually present in trout streams can also be found in this watershed. I recall my first experience with this river over a decade ago when I was amazed by the aquatic activity that I witnessed and the health of some of the resident fish that were fooled by my minnow imitation. The underlying beauty of the Grand is that it challenges your entire repertoire of fly fishing skills. There is not a technique or style of fly fishing that cannot be practiced on this river system. The question is where does one begin?

Let's start at the beginning of the calendar year and follow the hatches in relation to the fish in this magnificent fishery. The first major aquatic insect hatch, which affects our steelhead fishery from February through April, is the Early Black Stonefly (Taeniopteryx nivalis). It's the nymph stage that draws the attention of spawning steelhead and steelhead anglers. Early Black Stoneflies crawl out from their rocky, timber lodges, migrating to riverbanks, where they emerge into their adult form on land. During their migration towards the bank, steelhead encounter these vulnerable nymphs, and thus, the insects

Wild 16-pound steelhead with deformed back.

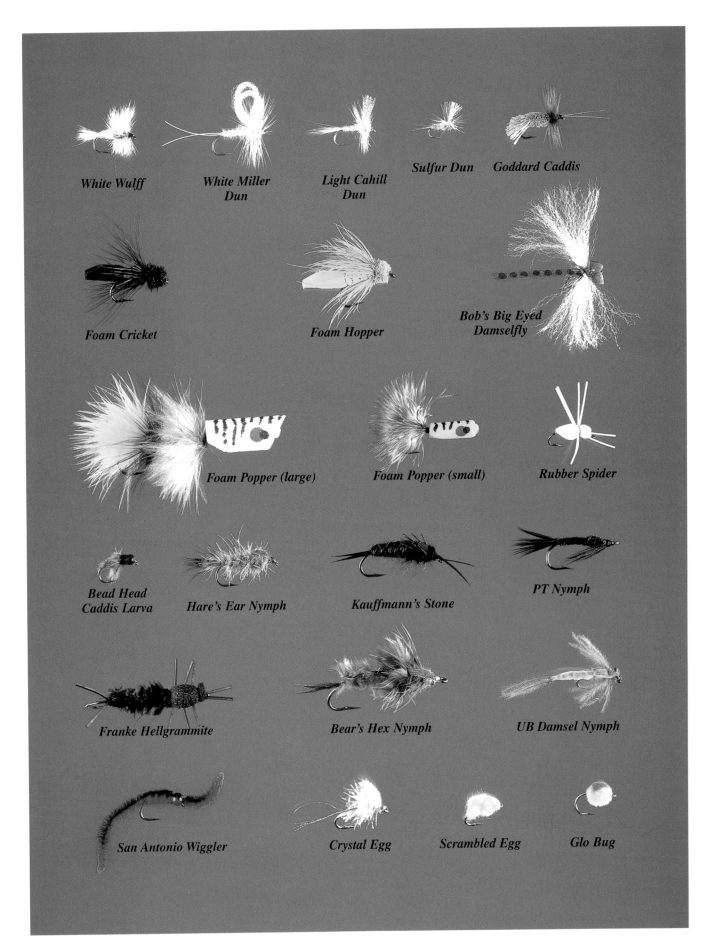

White Wulff

White Miller Dun

Light Cahill Dun

Sulfur Dun

Goddard Caddis

Foam Cricket

Foam Hopper

Bob's Big Eyed Damselfly

Foam Popper (large)

Foam Popper (small)

Rubber Spider

Bead Head Caddis Larva

Hare's Ear Nymph

Kauffmann's Stone

PT Nymph

Franke Hellgrammite

Bear's Hex Nymph

UB Damsel Nymph

San Antonio Wiggler

Crystal Egg

Scrambled Egg

Glo Bug

Taylor's River Bug

Woolly Bugger

Green Butt Black Bear

San Antonio Worm

Egg Sucking Leech

MC2

Muddler Minnow

Spoon Fly

TP's Tube Fly

River Rat

JB Special

No Body Matuka

Green & White Clouser

become part of the food chain. The natural is solid black in color, and a #10-12 Black Teeny leech will do the trick if you want to imitate one. These insects are also found in tributaries of the Grand which support spring steelhead runs.

This is the one time of the year that I don't mind having "bugs" crawling on me. Black stoneflies crawling on my hat and on the snow and ice lining the river are a sure sign that spring is coming.

Major non-hatch food sources present in this watershed year-round are the various species of resident baitfish. The fly fisher should not overlook shiners, creek chubs, dace, and other minnows, as well as, the darters and sculpins present in the river. All of the game fish that reside in the Grand continuously feed on the many species of baitfish because they are a vital part of their diet. Anadromous fish will also strike flies that imitate baitfish when they invade their territory. Streamer patterns probably account for at least 60 percent of all the fish caught on a fly throughout the season. White Woolly Buggers, or Nobody Matuka's, in sizes ranging from a #4-12 (weighted and unweighted) will keep a constant bend in your fly rod. Other fly patterns that work well are Mickey Finns, Black-nose Dace, Muddler Minnows and white foam poppers.

As steelhead season begins to taper off in late April, and the month of May brings leaves to the trees, the banks of the Grand change from brown to green. Mayfly activity takes wing as water temperatures begin to rise into the upper 50s. The first major mayfly of the season, which hatches at the end of May, is the Sulfur Dun (Ephemerella dorothea). This mayfly is also known as the Pale Evening Dun. This hatch emerges in gravel tailouts and riffles as warming water temperatures reach the mid 60 degree range by late afternoon. I have found excellent hatches from west of Lansing through the Portland State Game Area. This hatch usually signals the start of the bass season on the Grand. If you like to dry fly fish you ought to try casting Sulfur duns and emergers to surface feeding smallmouth bass. Another pale colored mayfly that takes wing in June is the Light Cahill (Stenonema canadense), which can be mistaken for the Sulfur Dun. They range in sizes from a #14-16 just like the Sulfurs and hatch in the same general vicinity as well.

I remember one particular June outing several years ago when I found both hatches occurring late in the afternoon. Smallmouth bass were making their presence known in the river where a long gentle pool swept into a wide tailout. I began drifting a #14 White Wulff with a #14 Pheasant Tail

Author's warm water fly box for the Grand River.

Battling a Grand River smallmouth.

Nymph as a dropper. After several successful presentations brought feisty smallmouth bass to hand, I noticed several slashing rises from fish feeding below the area where the smallies were taking my flies. I watched for several minutes as dun after dun disappeared from the surface. It was time to stop watching and start fishing. I began to strip out some line for a long probing cast. After several refusals I switched to the hatch-matching #14 Light Cahill and lengthened my 5X tippet. The very first drift resulted in a take and the water exploded as a drop-back steelhead made several acrobatic leaps into mid-air. My heart pounded and my disc drag reel began to sing as the steelie made several downstream runs. Minutes later, I was able to tail, revive, and release a beautiful rainbow trout on its way back to Lake Michigan. You never know what to expect on any given day when fly fishing the Grand.

One of the non-hatch aquatics of the Grand that plays a major role in the food chain is the crayfish. There are several species in the Grand and newly molted, soft-shelled crayfish are highly sought by smallmouth bass and walleye. Crayfish reside year-round in the Grand but hibernate during the cold winter months. As water temperatures begin to warm and reach the 50 to 60 degree range, crayfish begin their mating ritual passing on

another generation to food chain. All of the large predator species like common carp, bass, walleye, pike and catfish feed aggressively on these large freshwater crustaceans. July through September is the best time to present a fleeing crayfish imitation (#4-8 weighted) stripped along the bottom in pools and runs where large gravel and boulders can be found. Remember to stay in contact with the bottom. You may lose a fly or two, but you will also catch lots of fish.

There are two aquatic creatures in the Grand that can be a bit intimidating during close-up observations but they also play a vital role in the diets of the all the resident game fish in the river. I am talking about the Dobsonfly (Corydalis cornutus) and the river leech (Erpobdellas and Haemopsis). Both of these aquatics are large in size (three to five inches) and dark in color. The Dobson fly larva is known as a hellgrammite and they live up to their name by being very aggressive feeders in their larva stage preying upon other aquatic insects during their underwater life cycle. The hellgrammite is a secretive insect, living amongst the rocks and woody debris of the Grand, while leeches tend to primarily inhabit the weedy, slower pools and eddies of the river. Smallmouth bass are constantly on the prowl for both of these aquatic invertebrates and are quick to take them

25

when they make a mistake and reveal themselves. The best fly imitation to match the hellgrammite or leech is a weighted #6 Woolly Bugger (black or dark olive) fished along the bottom. One particular fly that closely resembles the hellgrammite, though, is a Franke Hellgrammite. If there is a fish within site of this fly, be prepared for a jolting strike from a hungry smallie on the prawl.

Terrestrial insects have their place in the Grand's food chain as well and imitating them will add to your successes on the Grand River. Flies that imitate grasshoppers, crickets, beetles, ants and terrestrial worms play a vital role in the fly fishers summer arsenal. As the Dog Days of Summer bring lower water levels and warmer air temperatures, terrestrial activity rises, bringing these land-dwelling food sources to the riverbanks. Excellent early morning or late evening surface action can be had until the cooling temperatures of fall set in. Concentrate your attention near the banks where there are overhanging trees and grasses for the best results. Rocky shorelines can also be productive.

The Grand has numerous caddis (Trichoptera) hatches throughout the year. There are too many to name, but the importance of these aquatic insects lies in their larval stage. The caddis larva is a small food source but just about every species of fish prey on these insects. If you like to nymph fish along the bottom, then you better have several sizes (#10-18) and several colors (cream, olive, green and gray) in your fly box. Many fly fishers add a dropper or second nymph to their presentation, and a caddis larva is a great choice. The caddis larva imitation is an important fly pattern during the steelhead and salmon runs due to the displacement of larva during redd building activity on the Grand.

Along with the numerous caddis hatches, dragonflies and damselflies (Odonata) make their presence known on the waters of the Grand throughout the summer. Green Darters (Anax junius) and Common Bluets (Enallagma ebrium) can be found buzzing along the surface teasing the resident fish all summer long. Both species have large aquatic nymphs that have to crawl out of the water in order to hatch into their adult forms. The nymphs of these insects can sometimes be mistaken for stoneflies due to their sizes (#6-12) and colors (primarily olive and brown) but they are better swimmers so don't be afraid to add movement to your imitation by stripping your fly back to the bank like the real McCoy! I have found the damselfly nymph to be one of my secret weapons for catching common carp in the weedy shallows of the Grand. And we can't forget about the importance of the adult in our selection of floating flies as well.

The last significant hatch to affect the Grand comes in late August and lasts through September. This hatch is known as the White Mayfly or the White Miller (Ephoron leukon). The factor which triggers this hatch is cooling water temperatures, signaling the coming of autumn on the Grand. Over the years,

I have taken full advantage of this hatch and I have learned a trick or two. Because the Grand has several pale colored mayfly and caddis hatches during the course of the season, most of the fish by this time of the year are conditioned to seeing white. So I pull the ole switch a rue on them. As the nymphs begin to emerge about an hour before dark and smallmouth bass migrate to the heads of pools and runs to intercept these insects, I tie on not a dry fly, but a small white foam popper (#12-14) to match the hatch. The action is fast and furious until you can't see your hands in front of your face. Fishing with a foam popper eliminates dry fly floatant and light tippets. On an average evening, one can land 20-30 fish in less than an hour's time with the help of barbless hooks

There are two aquatic insects that also need to be mentioned, but they are not found with much regularity or consistency in the mainstream of this watershed. Our two honorable mention mayfly hatches are the Brown Drake (Ephemera simulans) and the Hex (Hexagenia limbata). The brown drake is a much more important hatch on trout stream tributaries like the Rogue River, as well as Fish and Prairie creeks, but the Grand has sporadic Hex hatches during the month of June and into early July from Eaton Rapids to Grand Rapids. But the important element of this aquatic mayfly is the presence of their nymphs in the watershed. Their nymphs are some of the largest in the mayfly family, taking up to three years to hatch, so the resident fish population is very familiar with these aquatic insects. If you would like the opportunity to catch a common carp or a steelhead on a fly then these large nymphs better be in your fly box. My favorite Hex nymph pattern is an unweighted #6 or #8 Bear's Hex Nymph, and a smaller #10, because they imitate Drake nymphs well. I prefer unweighted nymphs so I can add just the right amount of sink putty or micro shot for a drag-free drift along the bottom where these fish are resting or feeding.

The Grand offers the fly fisher an endless amount of opportunities to pursue their favorite fish species on a fly

Grand River walleye like tube flies.

throughout the year. It is very challenging, to say the least, but all the hard work will make you a better all-around fly angler. Being open-minded and willing to learn and adapt to the ever-changing food sources is the key to successfully fly fishing this magnificent watershed in central Michigan.

∽ Grand Visitors ∽

During some years, there are modest runs of summer steelhead straying from other rivers during the summer when we have a spate of cool weather. When this occurs, the inevitable warm up sends these steelhead looking for colder water. The last time the Grand received a significant run of Skamania strain steelhead the best fishing was found in the Rogue River and Buck Creek. So when an angler hears about some silver fish jumping at 6th Street Dam in July after a cold rain, it will be a good idea to investigate the Rogue after the weather heats back up. Usually a few brown trout from Lake Michigan will also find their way to Grand Rapids during cool spells and will surprise the smallmouth and catfish anglers.

As the days shorten and the water cools in late August, the Grand River's anadromous season begins in earnest. Chinook salmon are the first species to migrate up the river. Having the river water temperature fall into the upper 60s seems to be the key that triggers the run. In most years this happens by the first week in September and may occur as early as the third week in August.

Currently, about 340,000 ready, or nearly ready, to smolt fingerling chinook salmon are planted in the Grand River each year. About 200,000 are placed in net pens at the mouth of the river where they are fed for a short time before release. The rest of the smolts are stocked at Riverside Park in Grand Rapids, which is upstream from the 6th Street Dam. While hatchery chinook are not fin clipped, studies have been done where tetracycline was added to their diet. This antibiotic leaves a mark in the vertebra of the fish. Approximately 40% of the chinook salmon

Dave Mahnke with a Fish Creek chinook salmon.

returning to southern Lake Michigan streams have been found to be wild fish. There is reason to believe that the contribution of wild fish to the Grand River run is even longer than realized, possibly because the amount of spawning habitat is much greater in the Grand when compared to the St. Joseph and Kalamazoo River watersheds.

Fly fishermen will find the highest concentration of king salmon in the rapids below 6th Street Dam. Fishable numbers will also be found in the riffles below the Lyons and Webber dams. The numbers of king salmon thin out further upstream,, but it is still possible to sight fish for kings in the upper Grand. Floating between Grand Ledge and Portland is a good way to find fish and the water is normally very clear in this reach in late September.

For anglers preferring smaller water, the Rogue and the Flat rivers both receive good numbers of chinook salmon, probably as the result of natural reproduction. Both streams have lots of prime spawning riffles and moderately deep gravel runs. Fish Creek also gets a dependable run of chinook salmon.

The king salmon run usually peaks in late September with fresh salmon continuing to enter the river through mid-October. Stragglers may show up as late as Thanksgiving but by that time they will just be surprise bonus fish hooked by anglers fishing for steelhead, yet some of the largest chinook of the season will be late-run fish.

Coho salmon begin their migration in mid-September, about two weeks after the kings first appear. While there is some natural reproduction of these fish the vast majority of the run is of hatchery origin. The Grand River receives the second largest stocking of coho salmon yearlings in the state. Only the Platte River, our brood-stock stream, receives a larger number of fish. In recent years almost 400,000 cohos have been planted in Lansing along with a small additional plant of 20,000 below Lyons Dam.

These silver salmon live up to their name and enter the river in bright-silver condition. They quickly find the fish ladders at each dam and make it to Lansing, a distance of 145 miles, still in very good condition. The females, especially, still have lots of shine when they arrive in the capital city. During the early days of salmon runs, a frequent report in early October is often that an angler fishing in Lansing has caught two salmon and a steelhead. The proper interpretation of this fishing result, though, is that the angler landed two red-sided male cohos and one silvery female salmon.

There is a two-week window of good coho fishing at Grand Rapids, usually during the last half of September. Fishing opportunities last longer at the upstream dams at Lyons, Webber and Portland. The plant at Lyons holds some fish there and there is trapping of some fish by dam configurations at Webber and Portland. At Webber, a grating was placed on the cofferdam to prevent the fish from missing the ladder opening and ending up below the turbines. The grate has been ineffective at keeping

Coho Salmon

the fish from going upstream, but it does keep them from going back downstream, and thus, from finding the ladder. At Portland, a long wall separates the main river from a small power channel where the ladder is located. Lots of fish tend to linger below the dam in the main flow because of this.

Despite these obstacles, lots of coho salmon make it to Lansing where they provide good fishing all through the month of October. Fish are concentrated below both the North Lansing and Moore's Park dams. The Red Cedar also receives a large run of these fish. The reason is that many of the salmon became imprinted to the Red Cedar when they were stocked. Typically the cooling water discharge at the Moore's Park Dam will make the Grand River uncomfortably warm for the young salmon at planting time. But before they leave for Lake Michigan, many move into the cooler Red Cedar where they linger and become imprinted. In addition, early returning fish will also move into the Red Cedar when they arrive in the fall because it is cooler.

Coho salmon prefer to spawn in smaller streams so they are attracted to many tributaries along the mainstream. Fishing for them just off of the mouths of these streams can be a good plan. Sycamore Creek, a small stream that flows into the Red Cedar in Lansing, is a classic example. This creek is large enough to fly fish as well, which is helpful because the Red Cedar is deep and slow at their confluence due to the influence of North Lansing Dam.

Brown trout are planted in the Great Lakes to provide fisheries near the shore. While none are stocked to provide a river run of these fish, a portion of these trout migrate up nearby rivers each autumn. Currently no brown trout are stocked near the mouth of the Grand River but that hasn't prevented them

from showing up in the river each fall. As this is being written, the Department of Natural Resources is proposing to begin stocking brown trout at Grand Haven in the near future which should result in a larger run of these fine fish.

A few brown trout will arrive upstream with the earliest chinook salmon and they will continue to run into November. Most brown trout spawn in October and early November. Surprisingly the vast majority of the lake-run brown trout stays in the river after spawning and the fish do not return to Lake Michigan until the spring.

Lake-run browns in the Grand River are bonus fish that are caught by anglers usually targeting chinook and coho salmon and steelhead. They are most concentrated in the mile of rapids below Sixth Street Dam, but they do ascend the ladder and are frequently hooked in the Rogue River and Prairie Creek. Their numbers are never very large, but they definitely spice up the action and sometimes they save the day when the steelhead or salmon are hard to come by.

Several years ago I was fishing for chinook salmon in mid-September with my daughter, Terri. We had fun catching several kings in the 15- to 20-pound range and were about to wade to shore and call it a day. One more cast proved successful and our departure was delayed as I battled another king. After several minutes of strong runs and violent head shakes, I got below the fish and was bringing it to the net. Just before it hit the meshes I discovered that my "king" was the largest brown trout I had ever caught. Terri got to see her dad get pretty excited and we posed the 18-and-1/2-pound fish for a bunch of photos before releasing it.

Every fall a few winter-run steelhead begin to arrive at Sixth Street Dam in September. The migration continues to build through October and usually peaks in November. Fall rains are a real key to bringing these rainbows upstream, though, these fish don't spawn until March and April so there is no real reason for them to run in the fall. Ample flows definitely facilitate the

Brenke Fish Ladder at North Lansing Dam.

Jim with lake-run brown.

autumn runs of these great fish. A common misconception is that the steelhead are following the salmon to feed on their eggs. This doesn't explain why these fish ran in the fall before the introduction of salmon. And, while steelhead will opportunistically ingest eggs that drift by, they hold mostly in the main river in deep runs and holes rather than below spawning salmon.

Runs of new fish from Lake Michigan dwindle as winter cools the water down to 32 degrees. Most of the steelhead winter over in the mainstream but if the autumn rainfall has been good some fish will be found in the tributaries as well. Mild spells in the winter may not trigger steelhead runs from the lake, but they will cause fish to move around in the river and become more active.

The main run of steelhead in the Grand River occurs in the spring. When there has been enough warm weather to melt the ice in the river, things get rolling. Once water warmer than 32 degrees hits the lake, the spring run begins in earnest. This usually occurs sometime in March and the peak of the run usually occurs between the middle of March and the middle of April depending upon the severity of the winter and the timing of the spring warm up.

Usually the Grand River is a pretty unfriendly place for fly anglers in the spring. High, off-color water is the norm. Low-water springs do occur, and that can be a good time near the riffles and rapids of the main stream. But normally, the places to be for steelhead in the spring are the tributaries. They clear much faster than the main river following spring rains and snow melts.

The only mainstream stocking of steelhead smolts occurs in Lansing. The remainder of the stocking is placed in tributaries. Crockery, Prairie, and Fish creeks, as well as, the Flat River all receive about 5,000 smolts each spring. The popular Rogue River is stocked with over 30,000 smolts each year. Even though the steelhead smolts are planted in the Grand in Lansing, they provide a good fishery in the Red Cedar River and Sycamore Creek for the same reasons as the coho salmon described earlier.

All hatchery steelhead are now marked. Most have their right pectoral fin clipped, but some may have their adipose fin clipped and may be implanted with a micro tag. Fish have now been marked for so many years that all of the hatchery fish returning to the Grand River should be marked. Over the past

Fly-fishing the Grand.

A large, male steelhead taken on an albino egg-sucking leech.

Kurt Hylek with a Prairie Creek steelhead.

two seasons I carefully recorded whether the fish were marked or not. With a sample size of over 300 steelhead from below Sixth Street Dam, the percentage of hatchery steelhead was 57%. The good news here is that despite the Grand River being a warm water stream, over 40% of its steelhead run appears to still be wild. The reason is that significant natural reproduction is occurring in the cold water tributaries.

During the same two seasons, the number of hatchery steelhead caught in Prairie Creek was only 4% out of almost 200 steelies. This is surprising since 5,000 hatchery smolts are planted there each spring. Dr. Paul Seelbach ,of the Michigan DNR, surveyed the trout in Prairie Creek and estimated that the stream produces 3,000 to 4,000 steelhead smolts each year. Obviously, wild steelhead smolts are surviving to become returning adults at a much, much better rate than their hatchery brethren. Releasing all of the wild steelhead that you catch will obviously enhance future runs of these great fish.

In general, the earlier runs of steelhead will occur in the tributaries closer to Lake Michigan. Thus, Crockery Creek will receive runs of spring steelhead from the lake before the Rogue River and Prairie Creek. These timing differences are very slight and there will be lots of overlap. The Rogue always seems to have some of the latest runs. This may be just because it receives the largest run of steelhead of all the tributaries.

A bright, hen steelie on the fly.

Large Laker on a fly.

The Rogue River is a prime fly fishing venue for steelhead in the spring because of the nature of the stream and the run it receives. Fish stack up below the dam in Rockford and in the deep riffles and runs in the first mile below it. This is not a secret fishery and it can be elbow to elbow during the peak of the spring run. If you are not into combat fishing the solution is to move downstream where there will be fewer fish but also fewer anglers. Access can be found at one of the five bridges between Rockford and the mouth. Even though the steelhead will not be as concentrated, they often will be more in the mood to grab your fly and there will definitely be more room for casting.

The last migratory species to arrive at Sixth Street Dam in the fall is the lake trout. The first fish will show up usually around the middle of October. Halloween is the traditional peak time for these fish but in recent years they have tended to run later and in fewer numbers. Nobody knows for sure why these fish run up southern Lake Michigan tributaries in good numbers. They are supposed to spend their lives in the lake and spawn on rocky reefs. These fish do spawn in the Grand River and their run coincides with spawning time in the Big Lake. Perhaps the reason is that there is a paucity of spawning reefs in southern Lake Michigan.

Lakers rarely ascend the ladder and some even seem reluctant to swim over the first cofferdam. Thus, the rapids area below the Sixth Street Dam is the place to find them. They prefer the slower, deeper water and can really keep you busy when they are in the river in force. Their presence is especially welcome when the steelies are scarce or are not hitting.

⟨⟩ Gearing Up For The Grand ⟨⟩

With over 250-plus miles of mainstream, tributary and arterial waters, choosing the proper fly tackle to effectively fish the Grand is a matter of personal preference. You need to select a location to fish, considering the species that you may encounter, so that you can equip yourself with the right arsenal of gear. This diverse river system contains just about every Great Lakes game fish available to the modern fly fisher. So, selecting the right fly tackle depends upon the quarry you target on a given day.

Let's begin the selection process with our fly fishing outfit. Three- to five-weight rods are a fine choice for stream trout, panfish and the addition of light tippets. Six- to eight-weight rods are the most commonly used throughout the course of the season for steelhead, smallmouth bass, common carp, walleye and catfish. If you are interested in casting larger flies to large fish like salmon, northern pike and largemouth bass, then a nine-weight rod is needed. The rod length is also very important when determining what to use. If you are planning to fish one of the smaller tributaries, then a seven- to nine-foot rod will do the job but if you are headed to the mainstream, I recommend a 9- to 10-and-1/2-foot rod which will give you better line control and distance. Your fly reel should have a smooth drag system, along with an external palming surface on the

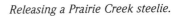

Releasing a Prairie Creek steelie.

Author, Jim Bedford, with a Lansing steelhead.

spool, so that you can apply additional drag when needed, and it should properly match the rod's line weight to balance the outfit. Spare spools loaded with optional line systems allow you to adapt to ever-changing fishing situations. I primarily fish with a weight-forward floating line and a slow-sinking intermediate line. Each spool has at least 75 to 100 yards of backing so that you can land that trophy fish of a lifetime. Leaders will vary in length from five to 14 feet depending on water clarity and desired presentation. The tippet material of choice is fluorocarbon because it's strong, abrasion resistant, and has the ability to disappear in water. You'll need several spools ranging from 0X to 6X (2-12 lb.). These will just about cover any fishing situation in the Grand.

The Grand is a year-round fishery for those willing to adapt to the seasonal conditions. Wearing the proper apparel and wading gear is also vital to one's success. Your apparel should blend in with your surrounding; bright colors spook fish and don't conceal your silhouette. Staying warm and dry are key elements during the cold weather seasons while staying cool and hydrated when the temperatures rise above 75 degrees will enhance your day on the river.

Neoprene or breathable waders with felt bottom soles, a wading belt and a wading staff will keep you safe and make wading heavy currents a bit easier. You still need to take precautions and wade smart. Polarized glasses and a hat are a must no matter what time of the year you fish. They are essential tools for reading water and locating fish. A vest or chest pack to carry your fly tackle and a landing net round out the slate for the essential gear needed to comfortably fly fish the Grand River.

～ Fly-Fishing Through The Seasons ～

Having explained a little about the equipment and gear needed to fish the Grand, I would like to take you through an entire year of fly fishing and explain the quarry and techniques used to catch the targeted species from season to season. Winters, fishing on the Grand from late December through mid-February, can offer some tough conditions like freezing air temperatures, shelf ice, anchor ice, snow and iced-up fly guides. But, for the cabin-fever struck fly angler, the chance to wet a line is worth the effort. Fall and winter steelhead are staging in deep holes and runs throughout the river waiting for the arrival of warmer water temperatures signaling the start of their spawning ritual. Pay close attention to the weather at this time of the year. When the thermometer rises above 32 degrees with the help of some sunshine, warm water temperatures trigger steelhead activity. During these periods, winter steelheaders travel to their favorite waters in search of some early season fishing. Dead drifting a small stonefly or Hex nymph naturally, along the bottom at the head or tail out of a deep run or pool, with a long, light leaders and enough split shot to tick the rocks on the bottom can result in a heart warming experience. Connect your tippet material with a blood knot and leave one of the tags to clip your slit shot onto. This trick allows you to make weight adjustments quickly and easily.

Another fishery that is overlooked at this time of the year, due to the elements and lack of how-to information, are the trophy river walleye and northern pike which can be caught on the fly until the closing of the season in mid-March. Walleye and pike, too, are sensitive to fluctuating water temperatures. A short warm spell can put these predators on a pre-spawn feeding spree. Migratory movements usually result in good concentrations of fish below the many dam systems throughout the entire system. Schools of baitfish are corralled in deep pools and slots. Try sweeping a sink-tip line, a short leader (five to seven feet) and a weighted minnow imitation along the bottom with a slow strip and pause retrieve for the best results. This is a great opportunity to expand your streamer skills, and occasionally even a bonus steelhead may grab your streamer.

The most anticipated season of the year is spring because it means steelhead on the Grand. Melting snows and warm rains raise the water levels, which in turn bring heavy runs of steelhead to the mainstream and most of its tributaries. The heaviest concentration of fish to make their presence currently occurs at the first dam of the system at 6th Street in Grand Rapids. When conditions are unwadable, drift boat and jet sled anglers fish the center runs and pools near the dam. They employ a drifting technique known as the chuck-and-duck method, which utilizes a floating running line, leader, slinky weights and a fly. This line system shoots through the fly guides with little resistance, and enables the fly fisher to vertically drift the area without any line drag, or the need to make several false casts. As these magnificent game fish continue their journey upstream, to the place of their birth or stocking, the confluence of each tributary with the

Author, Tony Pagliei, with a Red Cedar River spring steelhead.

Late-fall rains bring spring runs to Lansing.

mainstream offers excellent traditional fly fishing opportunities with streamer or spey styled patterns. Slow-sinking intermediate lines, accompanied by a short leader (five to seven feet) and a weighted fly presented down and across with the speed of the current is all that you need to achieve a strike. To effectively cover the entire river mouth area, begin by making a medium distance cast across stream from the downstream side of the tributary. Allow your presentation to completely swing into the shoreline. Continue making this comfortable cast, but take a step downstream after each cast until you completely cover the pool or run. Most takes will occur as your fly starts to swing towards the shore. These are some of the most aggressive strikes of the season.

My favorite fishing scenario begins by watching the spawning ritual taking place in the shallow gravel runs above deep pools. The dominant male guards the female and the redd while smaller males try to aggravate and remove the dominant male. This situation poses some of the hottest action of the season if executed correctly. First, position yourself far enough upstream to make an effective cast downstream and behind the redd. The chuck-and-duck method is used in this situation with fluorocarbon tippet and split shop placed 24 inches above the fly on a dropper tag. If you can keep from spooking the dominant pair, a dead-drifted streamer, nymph, or egg fly, sweep behind the redd, usually result in a violent take from one of the less dominant but aggressive males. Stealth and patience are the key to success.

Leaves begin to appear on the trees, wildflowers blossom, and high waters from spring rains begin to recede along the banks of the Grand signaling the end of spring. Trout season is in full swing on all of the designated trout waters of the mainstream. Aquatic hatches take wing, now is the time to float a hatch-matching dry fly in the surface film attracting awaiting brown trout and rainbow trout. Light-weight outfits, loaded with a double-tapered floating line, a nine-foot, 6X leader, and a box full of dries, emergers and nymphs, will keep the trout

fishing enthusiast busy well into September. The end of May offers the warm water fly fisher the chance to pursue smallmouth and largemouth bass on the fly, because both species have just completed their spawning cycle. There is no better time to take bass on a wide variety of flies; this is caused by their aggressive post-spawning feeding spree. Concentrate your efforts for smallmouth bass in areas of the river where large boulders and rocks are present in water depths of three to six feet. If you are looking for largemouth bass, search for weedy areas along deep pools and eddies. Surface patterns provide the most exciting action, and a standard weight-forward floating line with a seven-foot, 2X leader is all you will need to turn over most poppers or sliders. There is no such thing as a bad cast when presenting surface flies. Sound and movement are the triggers which will induce furious strikes. This is a perfect time to utilize a canoe or personal watercraft so you can cover miles and miles of river in a short period of time.

With the outside air temperatures reaching the 80-degree mark, the mainstream finally transforms into the awesome warm water fishery that many of us eagerly anticipate each year. Summer fly fishing on the Grand begins in late June, as low and semi-clear water conditions set in, and continues through the month of September. One particular species of fish, known as the Golden Bonefish of Freshwater, is becoming the most sought after quarry in the system during the summer season. Our quarry is powerful, intelligent, very wary, and has great eyesight and keen sound detection. They range in size from five- to 20-plus pounds. Their diet consists of aquatic insects, crustaceans and other invertebrates. And they can be found all across North America. Common carp offer a unique fishery to the warm water enthusiast ready for the challenge. Most of the carp in the Grand have finished spawning by the end of June and they too, go on a feeding binge.

Sight fishing for common carp is the ultimate stalking challenge on the river. Begin by concealing your silhouette with the

Kurt Hylek drifting a nymph to steelhead on Prairie Creek.

Fishing on the Grand River

natural background. Many fly fishers wear camouflage or drab-colored clothing so they are not as easily detected. You will find carp during low-water periods feeding primarily in shallow flats along the banks adjacent to deep runs and slots. They also like to seek cover in and around large sunken trees or dead fall near their feeding lanes. Once you locate some fish, then the stalk is on! Slowly wade upstream, and across the current, into the casting position. Polarized sunglasses are a must or you will never experience this great event. The technique is to dead-drift nymphs, terrestrial worms and crusteasans along the bottom. Long rods (nine to ten and 1/2 feet) with disc drag fly reels, drab-colored weight-forward floating lines, 10- to 12-foot leaders, fluorocarbon tippet (3X to 5X) and sink putty is the setup.

Make your presentation across and upstream with a slack cast then slowly pick up any slack line as you follow your fly through the run. When the line pauses or hesitates, set the hook and hang on! "Carp On!" is usually shouted after the hook-up by many of the local carp fly fishers on the river. You have discovered a new fishery that will hone your nymphing or drifting skills to a higher level.

Another phenomena takes place as well. While your focus is on shoals of common carp cruising and feeding along the banks, you indirectly tap into other fisheries. Smallmouth bass, rock bass, sunfish, catfish and walleye all eat the same flies that you are presenting to carp. During the course of a day, if you land a carp, smallie, walleye and a catfish on the fly, it's known as the Summer Grand Slam. Many anglers have achieved this warm water honor with great admiration from their fellow fly fishers.

Labor Day brings cooler temperatures to the river region and the late summer rains begin to cool the waters of the Grand. Smallmouth bass gather in small packs and feed on schools of baitfish throughout the river. Now is the best opportunity to take a trophy river smallie on a fly. Minnow-styled streamer patterns, fished just below the surface, will bring out the big boys. A basic stream presentation will cover long pools and runs that have large rocks and boulders present. Be alert to panicking minnows fleeing and jumping along the surface trying to escape their pursuer. White pencil poppers twitched erratically across the surface can cause some explosive late season topwater action. A seven-weight outfit matched with a

Grand River carp.

Smallmouth on tubefly.

weight-forward floating line and seven-foot, 2X leaders will turn over your presentation under most weather conditions.

The end of September officially signals the beginning of the fall season. The leaves on the trees begin to paint a portrait in the landscape along the riverbanks. The Grand once again magically transforms into a cold water fishery. Chinook and coho salmon enter the river system from the depths of Lake Michigan. These migratory salmon runs are the result of a lot of hard work over the years from the Department of Natural Resources. Natural reproduction is augmented through annual stocking by the DNR. The fly fishing community can't thank these people enough for all they have done and continue to do!

Our focus should be on following their movements in the lower sections of the mainstream and the tributaries. Seven-, eight- and nine-weight outfits with disc drag fly reels and plenty of backing are needed to land this large game fish. Traditional fly fishing with a floating or intermediate-sinking line, and strong leaders (0X to 2X) with matching tippets, are the norm for salmon. These are big, powerful fish that strike at flies out of aggression. The strategy is to keep swinging the fly in front of their face until you draw the take. They perform the

same spawning rituals as steelhead. The techniques stated earlier for steelhead will work for fall salmon too. Your steelhead flies also work in the fall as well!

By mid-October, as the salmon runs begin to wind down, lake-run brown trout and fall steelhead enter the lower section of the mainstream. Most of the lake run brown trout spawn below 6th Street dam while some stragglers make their way upstream into the Rogue River and Prairie Creek. Brown trout are fall spawners, so checkout the same gravel areas that the spring steelhead and fall salmon use to spawn. Dead-drifting techniques, fishing small nymphs and egg flies, work very well. Fall steelhead are by far the best quarry of the entire year. These trout are fresh and full of energy. One experience with a fall steelhead will have you hooked for life. Their acrobatic leaps and long, explosive, high-speed runs will put a serious bend in your rod as your disc drag sings a new tune. Their strength and endurance will have your arm aching before you can bring them to net or hand. Swinging streamers with floating lines and medium-length leaders (seven to nine feet) with long fly rods (seven or eight weight) are the required fly tackle needed to tame the savage beast. This fishery flourishes as

16-pound lake-run brown.

weather conditions get colder and colder by mid- to late-November. Don't be surprised if you have some of the most popular hot spots all to yourself at this time of the season.

Fly fishing the Grand River watershed is a never-ending sport because this river offers so much to the modern fly fisher. Being open-minded to the vast choices of quarry will extend your fly fishing season. Remember to practice catch-and-release and be a proud steward of this magnificent river system in southern Michigan.

‿ Catch-And-Release ‿

Most of the resident fish in the Grand River system, in addition to its anadromous visitors, make fine table fare and one should not feel guilty about harvesting fish for the table. However, releasing the majority of our catch will help maintain and improve the fine fisheries we currently have in the Grand River. Large predator fish like smallmouth bass, northern pike, walleye, channel catfish, and flathead catfish should be released. Keeping the two-pound walleye or channel cat for dinner and letting the trophy-sized fish go will result in a better tasting meal and better fishing in the future. We strongly encourage releasing

all wild steelhead and wild resident trout. And when keeping a salmon or hatchery steelhead for the table, try to choose a male for better eating and a minimal effect on natural reproduction.

Releasing a fish successfully begins with the catching. Never fight a fish to exhaustion. Use heavy enough tackle to subdue your quarry in a relatively short time. Take advantage of fluoro-carbon tippet material, which allows you to use heavier leaders while still fooling the fish. Try to pressure the fish from the side rather than lifting it to the surface. When lifting a fish, you are mostly fighting gravity while the side pressure makes the fish work harder and tires it faster. Follow the fish downstream when possible and get below it. This is especially important in heavy current situations. Trying to work a heavy fish back up to you will take a long time and almost guarantee an exhausted fish. Plus, by not staying close to and getting below the fish, you will also greatly increase the chances of losing it.

Always handle fish as little as possible. Small fish that can be controlled by grabbing the tippet can then be shaken free by grabbing the fly with forceps. If you must pick up the fish, wet your hand first. A net greatly speeds the landing of large fish. Use it as a corral and the leave the net bag in the water to minimize any abrasion damage or protective mucous removal. If you must beach a large fish, never drag it up on dry land. Find a shallow area where the fish can be forced on its side while still having several inches of cushioning water.

A pair of forceps or needlenose pliers should be a mandatory part of every Grand River angler's equipment. Manually unhooking a fish can be hard on the fish and your fly and, if the fish has sharp teeth like the trout and pike families, hard on your fingers. Barbless hooks also help, but even they can be stubborn at times. It can also be hard to pinch down your barbs after a big fish has dislodged a weighted barbless fly just before you bring it to hand or net.

Usually a fish will be ready to take off after being unhooked, but if it needs some resuscitation, always take time to do this. The best way to do this is by gently cradling the fish as it faces into a slow current.

Releasing the steelhead, smallmouth bass, king salmon, or carp of a lifetime can be tough to do, especially if you are fishing by yourself. The solution for easing the anxiety of letting a trophy fish swim away is to take a picture. A camera is always part of our gear, ready to capture a deer drinking at streamside, an eagle watching us fish, or a freshly caught beauty of a fish. If you plan to take pictures of your catch, always have everything ready before you lift the fish out of

October on the Grand in Grand Ledge.

the water. Of course, if you are taking a picture of yourself with the timer, this will be automatic.

Watching that big fish swim back into the currents of the Grand River or one of its tributaries is one of the most satisfying things you can do. It may or may not be caught again but at least we will keep its genes in the trophy fish pool.

Jim releasing a lake-run brown.

Double striper buck on egg-sucking leech.

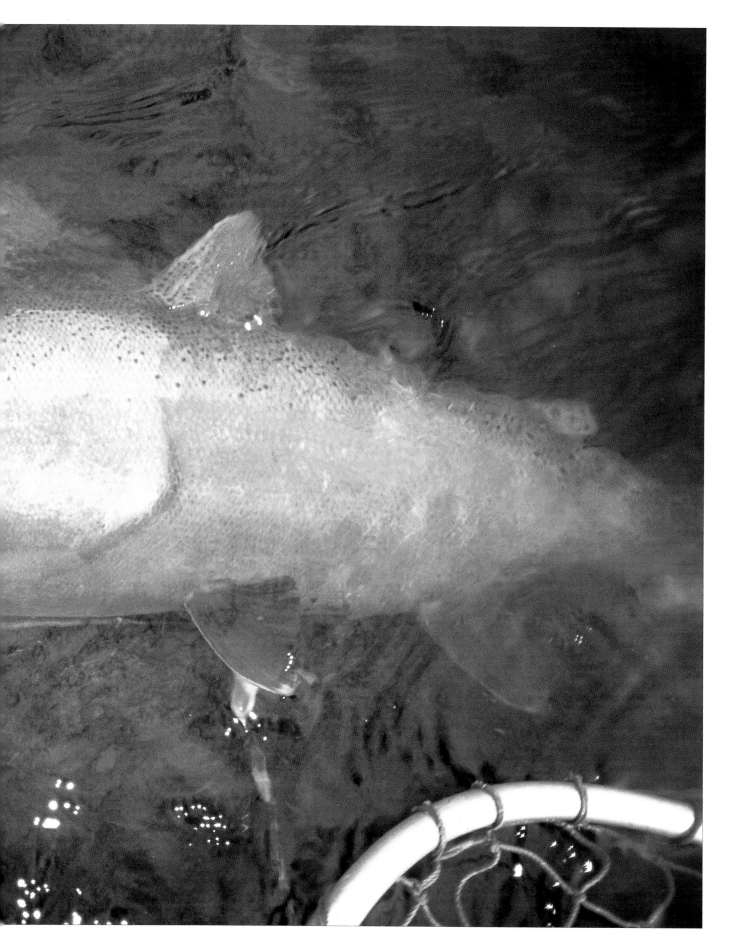

Fly Shops in the Watershed

M. Chance Flyfishing Specialties,
5100 Marsh Road, Okemos, MI 48864
(517) 349-6696

Grand River Fly Shop,
536 East Grand River, Lansing, MI 48906
(517) 267-1573

Great Lakes Fly Fishing Co.,
2775 10 Mile Road, Rockford, MI 49341
(616) 866-6060

Thornapple Orvis Shop,
1200 East Paris SE, Grand Rapids, MI 49546
(616) 676-0177

Angler's Edge,
Grand Haven, MI 49417
(616) 842-8588

Other Fly Shops in Southern Michigan

Macgregor's Outdoors, Inc.,
803 N. Main, Ann Arbor
(313) 761-9200

Hexagon Rod & Fly Shop,
2973 Midland Road, Bay City
(989) 686-6212

The Hairy Hook,
6650 Wellesley Terrace, Clarkston
(810) 623-1702

Benchmark Fly Shop,
32715 Grand River, Farmington
(248) 474-2088

Golden Hackle Fly Shop,
329 Crescent Place, Flushing
(810) 659-0018

Angler's Den,
8185 Holly Road, Suite 14, Grand Blanc
(810) 953-5530

Fly-Rite,
7421 S. Beyer, Frankenmuth
(989) 652-9869

Au Sable Outfitters,
17005 Kercheval, Gross Pointe
(313) 642-2000

Little Forks Outfitters,
143 East Main Street, Midland
(989) 832-4100

Beuter's Outdoor Ltd,
120 E. Main Street, Northville
(810) 349-3677

Fishing Memories,
8842 Portage Road, Portage
(616) 329-1803

South Branch Supply Company,
203 E. University Drive, Rochester
(248) 650-0440

Flymart Flyshop,
1002 North Main Street, Royal Oak
(800) 573-6335

Flymart Flyshop,
29229 Northeastern Hwy, Southfield
(248) 350-8484

Flymart Flyshop,
31009 Jefferson Avenue, St. Clair Shores
(810) 415-5650

Tackle Shops with Fly Fishing Gear in the Watershed

Al & Pete's Sports Shop,
111 S. Jefferson, Hastings
(616) 945-4417

Al & Bob's Sports,
3100 South Division Ave., Grand Rapids
(616) 245-9156

Arrow Shack Sports,
240 Bridge Street, Lyons
(989) 855-0200

Gander Mountain,
2890 Acquest Avenue SE, Grand Rapids
(616) 975-1000

Gander Mountain,
430 Market Place Blvd, Lansing
(517) 622-5700

MC Sports,
3160 28th Street, Grand Rapids
(616) 949-8510

Chambers of Commerce in the Watershed

Greater Jackson Chamber of Commerce (517) 782-8221
Eaton Rapids Chamber of Commerce (517) 663-6480
Lansing Regional Chamber of Commerce (517) 487-6340
Grand Ledge Chamber of Commerce (517) 627-2383
Portland Chamber of Commerce (517) 647-2100
Ionia Chamber of Commerce (616) 527-2560
Lowell Chamber of Commerce (616) 897-9161
Grand Rapids Chamber of Commerce (616) 771-0300
Rockford Chamber of Commerce (616) 866-2000
Ravenna Chamber of Commerce (231) 853-2828
Grand Haven Chamber of Commerce (616) 842-4910

Terri Bedford with a fall run Prairie Creek steelhead.

More Helpful Books for Fishing and Fly Tying

FEDERATION OF FLY FISHERS FLY PATTERN ENCYCLOPEDIA
Over 1600 of the Best Fly Patterns
Edited by Al & Gretchen Beatty

Simply stated, this book is a Federation of Fly Fishers' conclave taken to the next level, a level that allows the reader to enjoy the learning and sharing in the comfort of their own home. The flies, ideas, and techniques shared herein are from the "best of the best" demonstration fly tiers North America has to offer. The tiers are the famous as well as the unknown with one simple characteristic in common; they freely share their knowledge. Many of the unpublished patterns in this book contain materials, tips, tricks, or gems of information never before seen.

As you leaf through these pages, you will get from them just what you would if you spent time in the fly tying area at any FFF function. At such a show, if you dedicate time to observing the individual tiers, you can learn the information, tips, or tricks they are demonstrating. All of this knowledge can be found in *Federation of Fly Fishers Fly Pattern Encyclopedia* so get comfortable and get ready to improve upon your fly tying technique with the help of some of North America's best fly tiers. Full color, 8 1/2 x 11 inches, 232 pages.

SB: $39.95   **ISBN: 1-57188-208-1**

NEW YORK FLY FISHING GUIDE
Robert W. Streeter

Mention New York and most people think: concrete, sirens, and yellow cabs. This is true of a small area, however the Empire State also includes big woods, wonderful rivers, crystal-clear lakes, and great fishing. In this book Rob shares: the state's moving and still waters; species you'll encounter; access; fly plates, histories of the famed waters of American fly-fishing pioneers Theodore Gordon and Lee Wulff; general regulations; effective presentations; extensive list of resources; and more. New York State fishing has a fascinating history, spectacular surroundings, and varied fisheries, if you are fortunate enough to live or visit there, let this book be your guide. 8 1/2 x 11 inches, 113 pages.

SB: $19.95   **ISBN: 1-57188-157-3**

STRIPER MOON
J. Kenney Abrames

This is a beautifully written, all-color book about coast wade fly fishing (near the shore) for striped bass. Abrames explains tides and baitfish and covers techniques, reading the water, and the flies to use (shown in color and with pattern dressings). The author has a deep love and understanding of the fishery and I guarantee that you will want to fly fish for these wonderful fish after you read it! 8 1/2 x 11 inches, 48 pages

SB: $15.95   **ISBN: 1-878175-67-X**

SALTWATER GAME FISHES OF THE WORLD
Bob Dunn and Peter Goadby

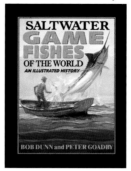

This is a book for all those who love the sea and the great oceanic and inshore fishes which inhabit it. It is a book, not only for anglers, but for marine scientists, nature lovers and seafarers of all nations who share a curiosity about these majestic creatures and how our knowledge of them slowly developed over the past two millennia. A 2000 year history of the early naturalist and fishes they first described. Illustrations are intensely evocative of the period and remind us of the skills of yesteryear, now largely lost. There is the never-told-before history of the ancient sport of sea fishing from its origins in the mists of antiquity to the present day. All color, 9.5 x 12.5 inches, 304 pages.

HB: $89.95   **ISBN: 1-86513-010-9**

VIRGINIA BLUE-RIBBON FLY FISHING GUIDE
Harry Murray

Virginia has a rich and vibrant history—President Hoover used to catch trout in the Blue Ridge Mountains to "wash his soul"—and a fishery to match it. The cool, clear waters of Virginia have much to offer the angler. Stream by stream, Harry Murray details their geography; the fish they hold; where and how to fish them; extensive resources; productive flies and presentations; and more. Virginia *is* for lovers—lovers of great angling in beautiful surroundings. 8 1/2 x 11 inches, 96 pages.

SB: $24.95   **ISBN: 1-57188-159-X**

HATCH GUIDE FOR NEW ENGLAND STREAMS
Thomas Ames, Jr.

New England's streams, and the insects and fish that inhabit them, have their own unique qualities. Their flowing waters support an amazing diversity of insect species from all of the major orders—in fact, at last count, Maine, alone, has 162 species of mayflies, the most of any state. Few, if any, books deal with the insects and life stages specific to New England, until now.

Hatch Guide to New England Streams, by professional photographer and "amateur entomology enthusiast" Thomas Ames, explores the insects of New England. Ames covers: reading water; presentations for New England streams; tackle; night fishing; and more. The bulk of this book, however, deals with the insects and the best flies to imitate them. Similar in style to Jim Schollmeyer's successful "Hatch Guide" series, Ames discusses the natural and its behaviors on the left-hand page and the three best flies to imitate it on the right, including proper size and effective techniques. Tom's color photography of the naturals and their imitations is superb, making this book as beautiful as it is useful. A must for all New England fly-fishers! Full color. 4 1/8 x 6 1/8 inches, 272 pages; insect and fly plates.

SB: $19.95   **ISBN: 1-57188-210-3**
HB: $29.95   **ISBN: 1-57188-220-0**

THE FLY TIER'S BENCHSIDE REFERENCE TO TECHNIQUES AND DRESSING STYLES
Ted Leeson and Jim Schollmeyer

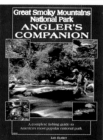

Printed in full color on top-quality paper, this book features over 3,000 color photographs and over 400,000 words describing and showing, step-by-step, hundreds of fly-tying techniques! Leeson and Schollmeyer have collaborated to produce this masterful volume which will be the standard fly-tying reference book for the entire trout-fishing world. Through enormous effort on their part they bring to all who love flies and fly fishing a wonderful compendium of fly-tying knowledge. Every fly tier should have this book in their library! All color, 8 1/2 by 11 inches, 464 pages, over 3,000 color photographs, index, hardbound with dust jacket.

HB: $100.00   **ISBN: 1-57188-126-3**

GREAT SMOKY MOUNTAINS NATIONAL PARK ANGLER'S COMPANION:
Complete fishing guide to America's most popular national park
Ian Rutter

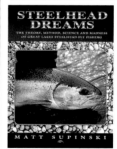

The weather, geology, geographic location, entomology, native plant life, and fisheries management policies have all combined to create daunting obstacles for the Great Smoky Mountain fly-angler. Now, Ian Rutter unlocks the secrets of this gorgeous region, including: trout streams, game fish, fishing methods, fishing seasons, catching larger trout, trout flies, and more. Some of the streams are closed to fishing for the study and preservation of brook trout populations, but those that are open to fishing are described individually, including fish species, productive flies and techniques, stream features, access, easy-to-read icons, and more. If you are fortunate enough to fish this beautiful, historical area of America, this handbook will be your perfect guide. 8 1/2 x 11 inches, 64 pages.

SB: $16.95   **ISBN: 1-57188-241-3**

STEELHEAD DREAMS
The Theory, Method, Science and Madness of Great Lakes Steelhead Fly Fishing
Matt Supinski

Screaming runs, big, thrashing jumps, relentless power—it's no wonder steelheading is an obsession for so many anglers. In Steelhead Dreams, Matt shares all you need to become a better steelhead fly fisherman, including: steelhead biology and habitat; reading and mastering the waters where they thrive; steelhead habits; techniques for all four seasons; effective presentations; tackle; plus best fly styles, casting tips, Great Lakes steelhead fisheries, tying tips, and so much more. If you are addicted to steelhead or look forward to becoming so, you must read this book to learn all you need to know about this wondrous fish and the techniques for catching them. Full color, 8 1/2 x 11 inches, 144 pages.

SB: $29.95   **ISBN: 1-57188-219-7**
HB: $39.95   **ISBN: 1-57188-258-8**

Ask for these books at your local fly/tackle shop or call toll-free to order:
1-800-541-9498 (8-5 p.s.t.) • www.amatobooks.com
Frank Amato Publications, Inc. • P.O. Box 82112 • Portland, Oregon 97282

0061